Secret Spaces

ENCOUNTERS WITH GOD IN THE HIDDEN REALM

ROMA WATERMAN

SECRET SPACES
Encounters with God in the hidden realm

© Roma Waterman 2022

All materials contained in this book are the copyrighted property of Roma Waterman trading as I Was Carried Pty Ltd.

To reproduce, republish, post, modify, distribute or display material from this publication, you must first obtain permission for the author at:

Roma Waterman
P O Box 288
Warrandyte Victoria
Melbourne, Australia 3113

roma@romawaterman.com
www.romawaterman.com
training.romawaterman.com

Published by: I was Carried Pty Ltd, Melbourne, Australia
Distributed by I Was Carried Pty Ltd

Writing, Editing & Design by Roma Waterman
Additional Design Joshua Hills at Roar Kingdom Creative

"For it is not knowing much, but realising and relishing things interiorly, that contents and satisfies the soul."

— *Ignatius of Loyola, The Spiritual Exercises*

CONTINUED...

THE DIAMOND SWORD   87

THE WHITE ARMY   99

FIREWORKS   115

TREASURE CHEST   125

THE ANCIENT FUTURE PLACE   135

CORONATION DAY   144

WINTER HIDING (POEM)   157

Contents

YOU CAN'T DANCE BY YOURSELF (POEM) 1

INTRODUCTION 3

EAGLE OF THUNDER 11

HIS MAJESTY'S THEATRE 17

THE HEART, THE SCEPTRE & THE CROWN 27

THE PIANO & THE GARDEN
(NO MAD HATTERS ALLOWED) 39

PARLIAMENT OF OWLS 47

THE GIANT LION 53

PAPA'S THRONE ROOM 61

THE DEEPER HEALING ROOMS 77

You Can't Dance By Yourself

There's a reason why you drag your feet
Why you sit frail
You cannot leap
Into the unknown or into divine decree:
You can't dance by yourself.

Frenzy is met by always running
Not to, but from
Who we are becoming
You might travel fast alone, it's true, but:
You can't dance by yourself.

There is motion, and it tricks us
Thinking any movement frees us
But moving solo is merely freelancing
When steps ordained were always made for two:
You can't dance by yourself.

You can't cross thresholds
Without the custodian
You can't pass through the gate
Without the guardian
This is not a Lone Ranger sprint;
It's a waltz for two

So don't dance the war dance alone
Put on your red prayer shoes
Click your heels
It's time to come home
Being strong means letting go
Let him lead - you just follow
And never, ever forget:
You can't dance by yourself.

Jer 31:4 (MSG)
And so now I'll start over with you and build you up again...
You'll resume your singing,
grabbing tambourines and joining the dance."

Introduction

Some people read.
Some people hear.

I see.

God is in the words. His voice is one of many waters. He can also pull back velvet curtains to release panoramic views of His presence. He is music; He is lyrics. He is grand theatre. However God speaks to *you*, it is all glorious.

When I think of the many ways God speaks, I am thankful for the times I have met with Him in dreams and personal encounters. And it makes me realise something deep at my core...

One of the best gifts I can give you is my stories of my encounters with Him.

Stories that help you see further than your own and help you enter your own story.

I have experienced this more deeply this year as I have studied the more contemplative traditions at Bible College. One ancient tradition that stands out to me is what I have been experiencing for many years without realising it – *Ignatian Meditation.*

It was St Ignatius of Loyola and his practice of Ignatian Meditation that has given language and, dare I say it, 'permission' for the encounters I have experienced over the last two decades.

The idea of Ignatian contemplation is the belief that God can speak to us through our imagination. Used to contemplate the stories in the gospels, instead of reading 'about' what happened, we use our creative vision to enter the story.

We are the blind man; we are the disciples, we are Jesus. What does the story look and feel like when we are part of the story rather than just mere observers? It is both impacting and revelatory.

Father David M Stanley, in his book *I Encountered God: The Spiritual Exercises with the Gospel of St John* explains it this way:

"... Christian contemplation is not merely an exercise of pious imagination: it is the quintessential means of relating in faith to 'the crucified Majesty of God."

Father James W Skehan enhances this thought by saying: *"Ignatius encourages us to engage the imagination and the feelings in our conversation with the Lord."* (Place Me With Your Son: Ignatian Spirituality in Everyday Life).

These stories you find here were so real I felt they were actually happening. Some are dreams I have had when I have been asleep. Others are internal visions I have received in prayer. And some are visionary encounters that have marked me for life.

These chapters are my private journals of dreams and personal encounters I received personally from the Lord over the last 20 years. They are but a portion of my experiences – which I hold dear to my heart. They have helped me draw close to God in ways I cannot express.

As you read them, I pray that they will encourage and inspire you to experience His presence not just theologically but visually. May the imprint linger in your mind and your heart and allow you to feel more deeply in love with Jesus – the centrepiece of our affection.

He wants to meet with you today, in the secret spaces, so that you may encounter Him in the hidden realm of His glory!

Thank you for going on the pilgrimage with me. I pray that as you *enter my stories, it will inspire you to enter your own...*

Eagle of Thunder

The colours of peacock all green and aqua with black hues glistening in the sunlight.

This is the giant bird I ride.

Starting at the top of the mountain, its ragged hanging cliff the launching place for the eagle of thunder to take flight.

I jump on barefoot, my leathered feet sinking into soft and aged feathers.

Grabbing hold of its leather harness, I launch forward as an address to the bird and sky to launch it and my body into the clouds. The sound his wings make cracking against the silent wind like thunder in the sky.

Jesus is next to me.

The wind falls gently on my face as I fall into its thermal waves. Summery, salty, cool and refreshing, we launch into the pale blue sea of sky.

Up and down, we lull and heave. I am flying over mountains of glory and deserts of mercy. The rhythm of the dip and rise refreshing my spirit. The laugh of papa as he watches my delight is as music dancing in the air.

And now the race is on. He says: *"I dare you to chase after me!"* And at the speed of lightning, He flashes ahead. All along, the music of his laughter guiding me to where He is.

My bird follows at my command. So fast and powerful, but there is no fear in me. I cannot fall, and I can't get hurt in this secret place.

I know I can catch him if He lets me. But for now, He just wants to have a bit of fun.

His Majesty's Theatre

The majestic theatre was brewing with anticipation.

Its red velvet seats, with their swirled gold patterns, echoed another era, rich with renaissance. Its seven tiers marked with ivory carvings and breathtaking architecture that is almost too much for the eye. This was a theatre with history, a place where artisans could come and share their story and be inspired by their surroundings.

But this is no ordinary theatre.

It is not of this world, for it is a place in Heaven.

Overflowing with people, the concert has already begun. Every single being is engaged with what is happening on the platform.

Whether the heat emanates from the crowd or from a spiritual presence, I cannot tell – for both are there and are as one.

Each tier is full of glowing faces, either standing or sitting on the edge of their seats, expectant and joyous. In the highest row, a brilliant light emanates the entire semicircle. It is hard to focus, but once I do, I realise that it is full of warring angels, standing tall, their wings outstretched, all looking down upon the humble stage on which I stand. They, too are engaged, and unified with all who are here.

Above them, there is no ceiling. An open sky covers us all. Our dome is a brilliantly clear night, sparkling with silver stars.

On the platform, I stand with many others. Our arms outstretched, our hearts beaming with love for the host that is in our midst. All of us on this Heavenly platform are wearing red velvet that accentuates our rich surroundings.

As I view this celestial crowd, I almost cannot take it all in. From left to right, I scan the breathtaking view. As my eyes reach the centre, I see why we are here. Why we have all gathered in praise and joy.

Sitting before me, in their majestic thrones, I see two strong men – one is called the King of Kings, and the other is my Father. This concert is in their honour.

Their faces are reflecting their glory and pleasure upon each member of the crowd. I see them clearly, and the love that comes from them is overwhelming. Gazing on their beauty, strengthening me at my core.

We are singing their praises in the noisy throng. Each voice is raised high, and the band is playing loud as we all lift our hands and extend our hearts.

"You are indescribable!" we exclaim.
"You are glorious! You are amazing, God!"

Each line we sing is heavy with love and adoration. The Father and His Son are pleased with what they hear. They are so enamoured by our love that they somehow inhabit our praises.

I have sung these lines many times, but tonight something is different. And for the first time, I understand that when I praise, God is ACTIVE. He is not sitting back, allowing my words to flow over him, remaining stagnant. God, as the great artist, is .... engaged. And as the great artist, He is watching over His word to perform it.

My word in melody expresses His power over the universe. Over the lightning bolts and the storms. As we sing, God lifts His right hand and sweeps it across the sky. As He does, there are flashes of lightning. Every few seconds, the crowd is lit up with each crash of thunder.

We sing about Him being the creator of the sun. He raises His right arm again, and the night becomes day as the sun streams its warmth onto each one of us. As we sing of His wondrous ways, He re-enacts each line for our pleasure.

I realise in a moment that my words are more than sentences pieced together to communicate a thought. When I praise Him, each word I speak carries a piece of the life of God. It is alive and more powerful than I could have ever imagined. It is creative and alive.

Our joyful song is coming to an end, but the crowd and those on the platform do not want to stop. With a shout, we lift our voices once more; our hands lifted high. We are overwhelmed by love for God.

As I look around again, my eyes are captured by the angels. I lift my head to see every one of them raising their right hands towards the starry sky. Each one of them is holding a silver sword that glistens in the evening light.

God is pleased. He loves His people. He stands from His throne to view what is happening before Him. Turning His head to each corner, He sees every person, every angel, hearing every note of praise.

One more time, before the great concert ends, He lifts His hand and sweeps it across the sky. As He does so, snowflakes fall on every one of us. The noisy throng rises again in adoration and delight as we outstretch our hands to capture these falling, glistening specks. They sparkle like diamonds in our hands.

This place is His Majesty's Theatre. This crowd is the great cloud of witnesses. This stage on which I stand is the church. The red velvet gown that I wear is the Holy Spirit. This is home.

As we the church sing his praises, all of Heaven is engaged with us. We are certainly not alone. The praises they sang hundreds of years ago still echo throughout time until they join with ours.

And God inhabits these praises, and actively engages Himself with His audience.

We share the song and the sword with all of history who have gone before us in the name of the King.

The Heart, The Sceptre, The Crown

The stark, dark room seemed empty. With no windows or doors, it was hard to see where it began or ended. The vast blackness seemed to go on and on, devoid of any light; it seemed one could get lost in shadows.

Then all of a sudden, a spotlight highlighted the centre of the darkness. I am standing in the middle, its glaring light showing every flaw and wrinkle. Not just the ones my skin have inherited but also those that have marked my humanity. It was as if this light could see into my soul so that nothing was hidden under its cold, blank stare.

I felt vulnerable. I wanted to hide, but all I could run to was the unknown darkness, so I remained frozen in position.

All of a sudden, the spotlight started to increase its perimeter. As it did, I saw there were others in the room. Three beings, walking back and forth in a circle, with me in the centre. They were staring at me, discerning my being, their eyes piercing into my harsh exterior. If I thought I could hide my innermost thoughts before, I certainly could not now under their authoritative gaze. Between them and the light, it was impossible to hide.

I squinted my eyes under the sharp beams, hoping to get a closer look at these curious figures. That's when I recognised who they were. It was Father God, Saviour Jesus and my friend, Holy Spirit. Immediately I relaxed, not knowing why I was there, but at least reassured that I was safe in their care.

They encircled me, walking round and round for what seemed like hours, then finally, Holy Spirit walked closer to me, disrupting the rhythm of their walking, and they all came to a halt.

He stood in front of me and, with gentle kindness, looked directly into my eyes. His gaze was piercing, not like spears to wound, but with laser power to burn the dross encrusted like coral around my weary heart. And then he spoke...

"Child, today we command every generational curse to come off you. The sins of the past will not be a part of your future. The health of your body and heart must realign today with the promises of God that have been spoken over your family since the beginning of time."

As He spoke these words, I began to feel a pulling, a tugging from my core. Something was coming out of me. Something that had been there a long time. So engrained into my being that the separation was like I was being cut in half.

In reality, those curses had been there for so long they had been hiding in what I thought was a part of me. I trusted Holy Spirit and allowed the process of separation.

As I stood there, different demonic spirits began to unwillingly tear themselves from me. They did not want to leave, but leave they must at the voice of the One.

As they separated from me, I saw them as they are. Ugly, vile creatures hiding in the darkness. The spotlight turned them to ash as they left my body, and they were gone.

My friend, Holy Spirit, stepped back into the outer perimeter of the light. Then Saviour Jesus stepped in.

He came close, his eyes were fire, and he looked deep into me. He lifted his hands and gently cupped my face. Close enough to feel His breath, He said: *"Now it's time for fear to leave. It's been there too long, hasn't it?"* I knew He was right, and I was ready.

He lifted his right hand from my face and pointed his pointer finger into the air. Suspended in time for a moment, there was silence and no movement.

Then he moved his finger with a quick flick to the right. Such a small motion, but at that moment, a spirit in the shape of my frame immediately stumbled out of my body. It stood staring at me in surprise.

As I looked into its eyes, dread came over its pasty frame. Trembling, it could not look at Jesus. But under that spotlight, he began to burn until he turned to ash, then completely disappeared.

Then just as my friend, Holy Spirit, had stepped back, Jesus did the same to make room for Father God. His white robe was luminescent under the light, his skin glimmering with glory, wisdom's beard draping from His sculptured jaw down past his shoulders.

As He came towards me, so much liquid love emanated from Him that it was almost unbearable for my sinful frame. I stood, trembling, as he looked deep into my eyes.

Quietly I said, "Father God, what will you remove from me today?"

He smiled and put his hands on both of my shoulders.

"Oh, my child, I'm not here to remove; I'm here to give you something."

I am surprised but wait in anticipation.

"My Child, I did not give you a spirit of fear. I did not give you a curse. I only give you blessings. I give you love."

As He spoke these words, He took his right hand and put it inside his chest. As He pulled his hand out, He held his beating heart. He then pushed it into my chest until I could feel His heartbeat vibrating through my body and pulsating in my ears.

Immediately I felt an overwhelming, supernatural love. Love for creation. Love for the creator. Love for humanity. Love for myself.

Father God spoke again, *"I did not give you a spirit of fear, but of power."*

Again He moved his right hand into his flowing white robe and pulled out a golden sceptre. It was made of gold so pure it was almost see-through. Inlaid with luminescent pearl, it had a golden orb on its top. He placed it in my hand.

Father God spoke again: *"I did not give you a spirit of fear but of a sound mind."*

As he spoke these words, he again took his right hand and pulled out a royal crown. Made of a silver frame, it was inlaid with transparent light blue sapphires and diamonds. He placed it on my head.

And at that moment, deep healing began to take place.

Suddenly, there was a movement to a new paradigm where long-standing illness, oppression and possession finally lost their grip on me and humanity. By releasing His freedom, he prepared His bride for war.

The Piano in the Garden (No Mad Hatters Allowed)

*I*t was a changing season. The sun is streaming through deciduous trees, dancing with the breeze. Spring takes off its shoes and begins to run barefoot on the summer grass.

I'm in the garden.

Here in the quiet, there is only Jesus and me. A long table is set before us, draped in ancient pure white linen. Hanging off the edges, it almost touches the grass.

Here, in the early summer quiet, I have entered a tea party.

Fine china teacups sit waiting for English breakfast tea to be brewed and poured. The high-spouted teapot was adorned with delicate orange and blue flowers sprouting steam, ready to be served.

Delicately folded napkins sit beside elegant tea plates amidst fresh, home-cooked delicious bites ready to be consumed.

The smell of jasmine and roses are in the air, not too heavy, but now and then, as the breeze dances, I smell their sweet-scented perfume.

Here at the head of the table stands Jesus. He welcomes me to a table prepared just for me.

His smile is warming, a glint in his eye and humour and wit is about him today.

He points far off in the distance over swaying trees and swooning roses. As I look in the direction of His hand, I see many people coming and going, each wearing long black top hats. All of them are trying to get into the garden. All of them want my attention.

But the Lord shakes His head and, in a thunderous voice, exclaims, *"NO! No mad hatters allowed!"* He smiles as he keeps them at bay, just at the sound of his voice.

He continues: *"Today, my daughter, you and I have tea."* With that phrase, He picks up the teapot and leans towards my cup. He pours from high as the black brew makes a dramatic entrance into my cup. The aroma carries a hint of lavender.

I make myself comfortable in ornately carved gold wood chairs with red velvet fabric.

As I sip my tea, the sun on my forehead, I hear peaceful birds chirp their joy in the distance.

Then the Lord points to a corner of the garden. He has a surprise for me. *"Look!"* He proclaims joyfully. He had saved the best gift for last.

A matt black grand piano stands amidst the jasmine and the roses. Regal and ancient, with beautifully worn ivory keys. Not the weariness from years of use but the wisdom of centuries that have played many heavenly sounds that break through barriers to reach Earth's ears.

"Come with me!" He says cheerfully.

Together we walk towards the piano. *"Now sit, my child."*

As I sit, my hands gingerly begin to touch the keys. I begin to play. I play from a place deep within my heart. It carries a sound of joy and hope and rest.

Jesus has a notebook in one hand and a pen in the other.

I am not alone, for we are writing together. There is an ebb and flow as He shares his ideas, and I sing and play them. There is no barrier between Him and me. The garden is a thin place, and I hear with no contamination from mad hatters or earthly bustle.

Now the song is finished.

"Child, will you play it for me again from start to finish?" the Lord asks.

I begin to play. As I sing, my voice joins the symphony of the garden. The trees clap their hands, and the grass sways to majestic rhythms; the birds are my orchestra. The flowers are my audience.

And Jesus, amidst the tea, cake and linen, is dancing barefoot to the song we just wrote together.

Here. Away from the mad hatters where dance, song and union collide with the divine.

Parliament of Owls

Today, after the airways had been cleared of demonic activity and the angels had dispatched across the Earth, a 'parliament of owls' could be seen descending into prime positions of government.

Heralding from the sky, these giant birds of PRAY flew into doorways as judges, premiers, prime ministers, and politicians entered.

These owls have been known to appear at pivotal times in history. Fueled with prophetic purpose, they stand at the pillars of each room. Others position themselves next to judges and lawyers or settle on the shoulders of leaders and whisper quiet truths into hearts and minds. Whenever they are present, the wisdom of God permeates the room, completely overshadowing the confusion and control of man-made schemes.

Difficult to see with the human eye, those attuned to the spirit realm have recorded their presence when significant shifts in government are about to take place. Today was one of those moments. The witnesses to their presence were the prophets.

As proceedings began, owls intercepted every snake lie and untruth - capturing them with their anointed talons and choking them until their death. The only words left hanging in the air were those that granted true righteousness and Godly justice to prevail.

And in a moment, deception was overruled, and the nation was primed and realigned for the purposes and plans of God to be made manifest on the Earth once again.

Witnesses said the owls could be heard cooing these words in the echoed halls of justice:

*"The Earth is the Lords and the fullness thereof,
There is nothing too impossible for the Lord!
He will restore the plumb line,
He will balance the scales,
He will rewrite laws and bring the justice the
Earth is groaning for!
Sons and daughters of man arise!
For He is God, and none compares to Him!"*

The Giant Lion

Early this morning, a giant lion was seen roaming the city's streets as its inhabitants slept. Cameras captured video footage of it calmly walking down alleyways and main roads.

Intermittently this great beast would stop outside certain shop windows to gaze inside. Its eyes were piercing as if a bright light was emanating from them.

Many shops were empty, some with signs on their doors showing foreclosure or bankruptcy. This great lion seemed to pause longest outside these shop windows. It is unsure how it knew which businesses were facing imminent end, but upon checking city records, the lion gazed with great intention into each and every one.

This tremendous yet gentle beast also lingered outside church buildings, occasionally standing up on its hind legs to place its paws and head on its front doors.

This tremendous yet gentle beast also lingered outside church buildings, occasionally standing up on its hind legs to place its paws and head on its front doors.

After several hours of roaming the dark city streets, the lion entered the central gardens. As dawn began to seep through the blanket of stars, he majestically walked up the steps of what is known as 'the shrine of justice'. Here is the highest and most central vantage point of the city.

In a majestic pause, he watched as city lights flickered in silence, waiting for the day to break. His face filled with compassion as he seemed to take in every street, every business, every church and every person that the threat of death and destruction had ravaged.

Finally, he took a deep intentional breath. Lifting his head, his golden mane flowing over his shoulders, he poised atop that high place and let out a deep, mighty roar.

At this moment, the greatest earthquake the city had ever experienced was recorded. It was a roar that shook the very foundations of the city. As people slumbered in their homes, walls shook. Governing lines in the ground carried the sound of this roar to the very far reaches of the city.

Not one square of land was left unscathed by this holy rumbling.

Then the dawn came, and the roar stopped. The lion looked over the city with pride. A realignment had taken place. Foreclosure and bankruptcy signs fell to the ground. Church doors spontaneously opened.

As people rubbed the sleep from their eyes and pulled open their blinds, a new day brimming with hope seeped into homes and hearts.

A new beginning was the only rubble the earthquake procured.

Since its sighting, some business owners reported seeing the lion's shadow as they opened their doors and turned on their coffee machines, ready for a new day. He is walking the alleyways of a city awakened to hope and prosperity once again.

Affectionately now called the guardian keeper of the city, we all now hope for a glimpse of Him once more. Something is different, and we know we will never be the same.

Papa's Throne Room

The streets to the throne room are familiar. I have run through them many times on my way to see my father.

Today is no different. I need to speak to Him, and I need to speak with Him *now.*

I am a little child full of ambition and urgency, and it never crosses my mind that maybe what I have to talk to him about is only essential in my eyes.

I run with all that is in me through golden streets. As I lean into its curves and rustic handiwork, it shines and glows in the light.

Sometimes, as I turn a corner, the road looks silver. It is so beautiful here, but because I run through them so much, I guess sometimes I take this beauty for granted. Besides, there's no time to stop; I've got to see Papa!

I reach the majestic cast-iron gates. They are guarded by two nine-foot angels at all times. They are wearing brilliant white robes, and each holds a silver sword between their hands in an upright position. Ready to defend if they need to, I know these angels know me because I come here all the time.

I throw myself onto these gates, animated and out of breath. I look these angels boldly in the face as I tell them: *"It's important! You have to let me in! I have to see my Papa!"*

They look at me, and in a second, I know that something significant is going on inside those gates, and they are not just going to let anybody in.

My mind's eye flashes to another scene—the throne room. And there is Jesus, sitting on His throne. He is a strong leader, a man who knows politics. He is a mathematician, and a strategic planner. I forget what an important man He is because I only know him as Papa.

He is sitting on the edge of His throne in great thought. Others are standing around Him, discussing life-changing events and making decisions that will alter many things in the universe. Losing their train of thought and needless interruptions would be uncalled for, unwelcome...and possibly even dangerous.

Instead of a wall, sheets of glass reach from floor to ceiling on the left-hand side of the room. They are monumental, and the view is spectacular. All the stars and vastness of space can be seen from those windows.

There are planets, known and unknown. Sometimes a shooting star flings itself across the blackness. There is the earth, grand, stable, fixed and seemingly ageless. There is not just one universe, but many. Galaxies that are yet to be explored, stars and planets unknown to humankind, yet God knows them all by name and daily tends to his galactic garden to keep it thriving, growing, beating with the touch of the life-giver.

And there is Papa. He is in an in-depth discussion with his colleagues. They consider strategies that will affect the earth. Are they talking about Russia? Iran? War-torn nations or poverty? They are intimately involved in working out a way to conquer the ugliness of sin.

The look on all their faces is not one that wonders if their plans will succeed. They do not merely have ideas. What they put in place, they know will succeed because God never fails.

Each elder listens intently to the Lord as he talks about His plan. As He speaks, He moves His hands in explanation. He points to a planet; it moves.

He reaches out his left hand towards the window and somehow cradles the earth. He brings His right hand down over the top of the earth, and as he does this, He carries the light of heaven with it.

This light touches certain areas on this fragile globe, and as it does it illuminates with the touch of God. Something is happening in real-time when He does this, but what it is, I do not know because I am just a child.

But I am still back at the gate, staring down the angels.

"You have to let me in!!! I need to talk to Papa!" I exclaim.

Somehow, although they do not speak with their mouths, they communicate to me that it's not the right time to meet with Him. But I'm not going anywhere. I have a sense of urgency, and of course, no child likes to be told they can't do what they really want to do.

The scene flashes back to the throne room.

As I wait outside, shaking those formidable gates with my tiny hands, I see my Papa in deep thought. He is holding his hands up towards the windows, in deep discussion, as He points to the cosmos.

Every eye of every elder is directed by His hands. They watch intently, clinging to every word and intent coming out of the mouth of the King of Heaven.

But then my Lord stops in mid-thought. Motionless, the expression on His face changes. Slowly He turns His head to the right of the room.

Twenty-foot golden doors are closed and locked, so there would be no interruptions. He looks towards these doors. Then He looks towards the elders.

He drops His hands and says to them, "Please excuse me for a moment; I can hear my little girl calling."

With that statement, He stands from His throne and walks towards the doors. They slowly begin to open as He walks towards them.

Even His thoughts are powerful in this place, He just has to think of what He wants, and it happens! The doors open, and He hurriedly walks through them.

As this is happening, I am still standing at the cast-iron gates. I am shaking them, pleading my case to the angels.

But then, suddenly, the gates begin to open. The angels stand back – a sign that I can walk through.

I run past the angels and the gates...

I run through the garden that encases the throne room...

At another time, I may have stopped and marvelled at the beauty of this place. But now, I am on a mission.

I run through to the front door that is already open...

Before me stands a vast white marble hallway.

No royalty on earth owns a palace as grand and beautiful as this palace. Pillars reach up to the thirty-foot ceilings and curve into the roof. They are carved with stories from the ages of great men and women who trusted in their God. Even the handiwork of heaven testifies to the goodness of God.

I run through the hallway. As I am doing this, my Papa is coming through the golden doors from the throne room. I see him at the end of the hallway. I'm delighted to finally see Him!

I run towards Him...

He sees me, smiles and begins to run towards me.

Finally, we engage.

We collide, and He lifts me up and throws me in the air. He laughs and cradles me in His arms and tickles me.

Gently, He carries me back to the throne room.

Back to the elders...
Back to the expansive view of space...

We sit back on His throne, and He cradles me on his lap. I sit there, safe and secure.

He does not ask me what I need to talk to Him about. I do not tell Him, because I can't remember.

Every now and then, I tell Him something. It's probably of no real importance, yet He listens to me as intently as He listens to the elders.

He continues His discussions with those in the room.

He trusts me and speaks openly with them, not minding that I can hear all His secrets and all His plans.

After this meeting, we might go and have a look at the gardens.

I will ask Him in a minute……

Because He is my Papa, and I know I can ask Him anything.

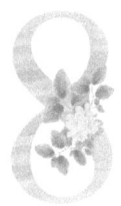

The Deeper Healing Rooms

"Just wait here, and someone will be with you shortly."

The angel smiled as he left me alone in the entrance to the great library. His luminescent wings are barely visible against the bright tunic loosely wrapped upon his celestial body.

I always love coming to this place. Even though grand in design and size, it has a sense of comfort and peace.

From the entrance, I could see the many shelves of books reaching to the glass ceiling above. As the light streamed pillars to the polished wooden floors, I lovingly gaze at the thousands, maybe millions of books here.

Each book was lovingly considered by the great philosophers. Books written on earth that were held dear to the Father's heart were placed here. Some were history books, some were others children's stories. None more important than the other.

Some 100 years old, others, more than thousands. Some still hidden in the recess of earths belly, not yet discovered by human hands, yet the words embedded and precious to Heaven's heart, waiting to be revealed to the hearts of man.

There were other people here, flicking through pages, sitting cross-legged on the floor, drinking in stories from before their time.

Angels walked these halls, shuffling books from one place to another, arranging systems, and helping those who were new here.

I walked over to the brown leather couch to sit and wait. My garments were those you would wear to go into surgery. Unlike the others who had come here to read,

I was awaiting an operation.

When I had prayed for healing for my body, this is where the Lord took me. One moment I was on my knees; the next, I was transported to this secret place. I waited for further instruction and felt at complete peace. I knew if I was here, everything was going to be taken care of.

After a while, I was greeted by another angel. I do not know his name. *"Hello, I have been assigned to take you to the deeper healing rooms. Please follow me"*. He speaks gently.

I have been to the healing rooms in Heaven before, but these rooms were different. They were for those who needed specific healing that required detailed knowledge, understanding, and skill.

I followed the angel into what appeared to be a large observatory. Just off from the great library, I wondered why it was not in the healing quarter. I looked across the room. The ceiling was made of glass, and light streamed through.

What looked like beds made of black stone were lined in an orderly fashion across the room. At many of these beds, people were lying on them, a sheet over their torso. Angels stood over them. Some had books in their hands as if they were reading some piece of vital information that could help them.

"Welcome to the healing rooms; please, lie down here". The angel smiled at me and pointed to an empty bed. I lay down, and he lay a sheet over me.

Once I was comfortable, he hovered his hand over my body – beginning at the top of my head and going down to my feet. It seemed to give him the information he needed. He then raised both hands and hovered them over my stomach. As he did, I felt a heat enter that area.

He looked at me and smiled. *"The Lord is healing you; He is the God that heals,"* he said as he continued his work.

After a while, he walked away. Several minutes later, he came back with a large book in his hands. It was old, with thick, aging pages. I couldn't read what was inside, but the angel read intently for a few minutes. Holding the book in his left hand, he continued to wave his right hand over my body.

"I have done all I can here", he said after a few minutes. "Now, as the sun shines upon you, rest a while".

He smiled, snapped the book closed, squeezed my shoulder and walked away. As he did this, the light streaming from the glass ceiling began to shift and move toward me. Once it reached my body, it stopped, and I felt warmth and peace cover me. I fell asleep for what seemed like hours, but maybe it was minutes – it was hard to tell.

As my healing time came to an end, the sun began to move its position in the room. This woke me. I felt refreshed in ways hard to describe.

My healing was complete.

The Diamond Sword

She looks about 12 years old.

Somehow I knew, just by looking at her, that she was full of life, someone who loved to have fun yet still insecure and only beginning to find out who she really was.

She did not know how she got there, but she was not afraid. As she stood in the open desert, sand beneath her feet, the air was still. The silence was so loud it could only make her focus on her present surroundings.

She looked to the left and saw sand and sky, so she thought she was alone. She looked to her right, and that's when she saw Him.

He was crouching on the ground writing something in the sand. She knew who he was immediately. *She had known him all her life.*

As she gathered her thoughts, a flash of wind brushed through her hair. She was at peace and began to drink in where she was. *This man was Jesus.*

And she was in a scene from a story she had heard a thousand times before. This was the beginning scene of the woman caught in adultery.

Desert floor, Jesus writing in the sand – who else could it be?

In her youth, she thought she knew it all too well. She didn't need to know anymore. In her quest to see and hear new things, she began to walk out of the scene –to look for something more– something else. To search for something she didn't know.

She turned to her left and began to walk away. Immediately Jesus stood up and gently grabbed her arm. *"Not yet,"* he said. *"There's more for you to see"*.

Lovingly, he put his arm around her and pointed to the empty sand before her.

"What do you see?" He asked her as she cradled into His side.

As she looked up, she saw a woman walk into the scene—a beautiful woman with long dark hair wearing off-white flowing robes. Two men pushed her in front of Jesus. Her arms and legs were chained. She looked tired. Tired of life. *Tired of herself.*

The girl studied the woman.

As she began to understand the picture in front of her, she noticed more than what she had previously seen.

Hanging off the woman were demons—ugly green demons with long tentacle arms and legs. Like an overgrown vine, they wrapped themselves completely around her whole body. They would not let her go without a fight – she was theirs. Theirs to own, manipulate and control.

Again Jesus said to the little girl: *"What do you see?"* She looked at the woman and then up at Jesus. She did not need to say anything. Somehow He just knew what she was thinking.

"I want you to speak to this woman", He said.

The little girl looked up at Him – what could she say to a woman captured by the sin that had haunted her for years? What kind of peace or ease could she bring? She felt she had nothing to offer, ... *and so said nothing.*

"I want you to cast those demons out," Jesus said. His voice was resolute. He was not going to take no for an answer.

Because she loved Him, she knew she must do what he asked. Even though she did not understand, she trusted he would not ask her to do something if he thought she could not do it.

She looked at the woman.

With Jesus' arms around her, she spoke to the woman and cast the demons out. She was not commanding or authoritative. She was a child and spoke like a child. But she had faith to do what she was asked because He had asked her to do it.

As she spoke, the demons began to fall off her. One by one, they fell powerless to the name of Jesus. Eventually, the woman was standing free of all entanglement. All *her shackles were gone!*

Jesus then pulled away from the little girl and stood directly in front of her. He was proud of her.

From His robe, He pulled out a shining silver sword. It was majestic and ancient.

As He wielded it into the air, the wind spoke of its integrity and justice. Its mercy and kindness. Somehow the sword was alive and was heavy with the presence of heaven.

On the tip of this beautiful sword were bright, shining jewels. They were diamonds. They were pure and seamless. The little girl had never seen diamonds like this before.

Jesus pointed the sword towards her body. Without even thinking, she opened her mouth, and He placed the sword on her tongue.

He then slowly pulled the sword away from her, and as He did this, the diamond droplets were left in her mouth. He then placed the sword back in his robe.

The little girl closed her mouth and looked around. She looked to her left; she looked to her right. Instinctively, she opened her mouth. As she did, shafts of light pierced through her surroundings. Wherever she focused her attention, that light would penetrate.

Somehow she knew that things inside her were different. She knew something had changed within her.

God had given her a gift far beyond what she could have ever dreamed or imagined, and only time would tell what it would be for and how powerful it was.

The White Army

*I*t is springtime in the forest.

The air, awakening from its winter slumber, smells fresh and new.

The sun streams its shafts of light boldly between the pine trees onto the soft dirt ground.

There is a sense of a new beginning, new hope, and new strength after a long and refreshing rest. The winter has passed, and the time has come to fight.

Amongst the peaceful sounds of the earth's new birth stands a silent people.

Their horses are regal and restless, ready to run but being held back by their masters for the awaited time. Each person has scars of battle on their face and hearts, but none are beaten.

There is no defeated spirit. For here, amidst this secret place, stands a gathering of favoured people, chosen for a task more significant than themselves. A task beyond their own strength, yet none falters. This is none other than the white army, ready to fight and awaiting instructions from their king.

Thousands have arisen from the shadows, called by the still, small voice. They have come from the East, the West, the North and the South.

Some are women with fire and strength in their eyes. Others are men, young and old, ready to fight with silver swords sharpened by adversity. Many are young children who are unafraid and unashamed.

They stand in the centre of the forest, awaiting the visitation of their master.

They wait and wait, patiently, all facing towards the throne that will hold its king. It stands giant and solitary. On each side, there are three angels, feet spread apart, their hands on their swords' helms, and their swords planted firmly in the ground.

Dressed in white, they are beings of war, resolve in their piercing eyes. They, too, wait for the command of their king.

Amidst the anticipation, a rush of wind gently brushes across the scene—all who are gathered look up and stand straight, ready with anticipation.

Suddenly from the forest walks the great and mighty king. The one they have been waiting for.

He walks towards His throne; He turns His head and looks at the army set before him. He smiles quietly at the strength of his people but does not lose stride.

He walks up to his throne, but He does not sit. He knows He is king. He is comfortable with his titles. He does not need his throne to affirm who He is. He loves His people, and He is keen to address them.

He does not speak with words. Yet we all understand.

He looks at each one of us and knows us. This enough speaks volumes to us.

His heart calls us to the last great battle. The battle is not for land, justice, or peace. This is the battle for this and more. It is the battle for the human heart.

The battle to ransom the lost souls that have been taken by the evil one. These are the dark days, and they grow dimmer by the hour. It is time to recover what is His.

He does not need to urge us. We are ready.

With one look, He calls you out.

You walk up to the master and bow your head. His hand rests firmly on your right shoulder. You turn your head to see a nail-scarred hand. It gently pushes you to your knees.

You bow your head in reverence and wait.

The King of Kings pulls out a bright sword from his robe. Its gleaming blade shines in the sun, reflecting its brightness. Streams of light seem to emanate from it. *It's almost like it's alive.*

The Captain of the White Army lifts this sword high above His head. Artfully He lowers it so that it touches your right shoulder and then your left. He places the blade inside His robes and, with both hands, gently lifts you up onto your feet.

You have been given the highest honour. You are now a knight in the white army. You are ready to fight. And you do not take this lightly.

Graciously, you step back and join your fellow soldiers. The great one then looks over the gathering, ready to address them once more.

Again, He needs no words. He speaks to us without the need for them.

There is great compassion in His eyes as He urges us to fight for the lost ones.

It is only then that we comprehend these lost men and women have indeed been deceived by the prince of death. They are chained and imprisoned. They cannot see the light. They are lost in darkness, and it is time to violently take them back.... by force.

Even if it is at the risk of our own lives.

We understand that if they die in darkness, they are forever lost. Yet, if we die in the battle, we enter into a more excellent light. So we cannot leave them there.

We must fight for them.

With great strength and authority, the Lord speaks."*Go!*"

The master finally releases us. Every soldier lifts their sword and shouts His praise. We turn to face the forest. Suddenly the quiet erupts into a throng of battle cries.

The horses pound the dirt with their hooves. They begin to gather speed.

Some of us are riding on their backs; others are swift to run on their beautiful feet. We are all ready to move towards the battle.

And so it begins.

The thunder of the great white army is heard beyond the gates of destruction.

In the darkness, chief demons begin to feel uneasy. Where does it come from? What is this sound?

These evil hordes hear it growing with every second. And their fear rises up to meet their fate.

It gets louder and louder. Days turn into months; months turn into years. But we are the patient ones. We do not give up.

The prisoners wait and cry. In their chains, they wonder how long they will remain captive. They do not understand that their freedom is at hand. The darkness has blinded them and made them deaf.

But somehow, without them understanding, with every step forward the white army makes, hope begins to abound in their hearts.

Finally, we arrive.

We do not wait for an invitation.

The gates are plundered. They crumble at the sound of our roaring praises.

Demons flee and are stunned into motionless. Like deer in headlights is when darkness meets glory revealed.

The army overcrowds the festering cells. In gleaming brightness, they search through the darkness. Every crack, every crevice is looked over to find the prisoners.

Some find large numbers of them huddled together in their chains. There are ash and dirt on their faces. Blistering sores and jagged bones almost protruding through tightened skin.

They are beyond thirsty. They do not understand, yet they reach out for help.

Many cannot walk on their own. Even if the prison doors were opened, they would not have the strength to step into their freedom.

We lift them up onto our horses as we look for more. Some are alone, lying on cold stone floors, looking into deep darkness. They see nothing but hopelessness. A kind soldier leans over towards their faces, and their healing begins.

 So many of them! We take them all. We do not leave one behind.

The White Army streams out of the darkness, back towards the light, back towards the forest of hope. Victory is in their song as their voices rise towards the heavens. The prisoners squint as they begin to see the sun for the first time in years. Like cool water, peace washes over them.

And the battle is won. The prodigals return to their father. To be washed, fed, and made clean.

Once they have returned, in the final mark of victory, they are ceremoniously given white robes.

And like so many others before them, they kneel before their king. He pulls out his sword again and knights His new princes of war.

Passion rises within them. The desire to return to the darkness where they were once so lost. To find others. To fight for them, just as they were fought for.

They mount up on their horses and look to their master. Great love for Him drives them to return to the blackened prison where they were once held captive.

And the story begins again.

The battle is fought, the battle is won.... *and the battle is.*

11
Fireworks

one tired.

The kind of tired that makes your insides ache. The kind of tired where you can't sleep, staring blankly into space as nothingness washes over you.

I knew it was time to go to the secret place. *"Lord, I need to rest,"* I said. I close my eyes, lift my hands to the heavens, knowing supernatural arms will lift me to the healing rooms. I was sure that was where I needed to go. That was where I always went when it was time for refreshing.

When I arrive, I help myself to one of the beds, soft, warm, and comfortable. The atrium, with its triangular glass ceiling, opens up the expanse of heaven's sky, pouring peace into my spirit.

I climb under the sheets, already beginning to feel rest permeate my weariness. Candles lighting up the darkened room –maybe hundreds of them, made this such a peaceful place.

Then, the great physician enters the room. His eyes gleamed, complimenting the cheeky grin on his face. Not the kind of expression you would expect at this moment.

He walks up to me. With both hands, he cusps my face and looks me in the eye.

"Daughter," He begins. *"You do not need rest; you need to have a bit of fun!"*

My mind is trying to take this in. I just want to sleep! But I know He knows best, so I allow Him to gather me up in His arms to take me from this place of solace.

Immediately we are in a theme park.

"Oh!" I exclaim. "We are in Disneyland!" The Lord laughs. *"Oh no...this is better than Disneyland....come on!"*

We come to the ferris wheel ride. It is night time, and night festivities are about to begin. The sky is crystal clear, the scent of summer in the gentle breeze. The music emanates from speakers across the park – nostalgic, mystical, otherworldly. Sights and sounds married together to envelop all the senses. Nothing has been missed here; every detail is taken care of.

As we enter our cubicle, I see my family there. My kids are squealing with delight.

The wheel begins to turn, rising, rising, higher than I could ever imagine. I've never been so high! The sky drinking me up as I reach for its peak, of which there is no end.

Finally, we reach the top. The wheel gently jolts to a halt. *"We are here"*, Jesus says.

I wonder what He means.

He opens the cubicle door into nothingness. "Come on..." He says, ushering us to jump out. Surely he cannot mean to jump into nothingness. We could not even see the ground from here.

Because it is Him who asks, I trust. I gingerly step out. To my surprise, I am buoyant in the sky. I am dancing with stars, floating up and down as the wind holds me.

The rest of my family follows. Laughing with joy as we experience the feeling of weightlessness.

And then.....*the fireworks begin.*

Instead of watching from the ground, we entered the fireworks. How this is possible, I do not know. We are in the midst of this light show: colours of red, yellow, greens, blues and brilliant whites. Explosions of mercy, joy, healing and grace. We are not spectators; we have entered the sights and sounds of a work of art hanging and moving in the sky.

But these are no regular fireworks. As a flash comes towards me, it goes through me. Right into my belly. As it touches my core, it wriggles through all my senses, tickling me from the inside out, and releasing uncontrolled laughter. It is impossible not to laugh when they reach your centre.

I watch as my family experiences the same thing. Waiting for the moment, yet the flash is unexpected and quick when it comes, making it all the more fun.

Another flash, another colour reaches for my son. As it hits his little body, it thrusts him across the reach of sky, much like a father throwing a child up in the air. He squeals with delight. The music of laughter is filling the air, mingling with the sounds of pops and explosions as more fireworks fill up this starry night.

We are either laughing or being flung across the air, feeling our bellies rise and fall in this 'fireworks ride'.

Today, rest looks like fun. It might be time for ice-creams and popcorn soon.

The kids will love that.

12
Treasure Chest

I lay my head to sleep.

As my eyes close to the physical world, the not-seen suddenly appears, and I enter another realm.

I am in the secret place in heaven.

This time, I have entered a secret room carved out in a vast rust-coloured rock that overlooks the valleys of heaven.

I can see many windows into many other rooms carved into the formidable rock. At this moment, Jesus is with me in this private room. It is filled with peace and rest. I am sitting in an armchair, looking out at the breathtaking view. Jesus is sitting next to me.

"Child," He says lovingly. *"Look at me."*

Disrupting my view, I look into the eyes of my Beloved.

As I do, He leans in, lifting His hand to supernaturally enter my chest. I can feel the pull as His hand enters my heart. It is a strange, inexplicable sensation.

Jesus pulls out of my heart an old, beautifully ornate tin box. He then places it on His lap and opens the lid, balancing on creaky, rusty hinges. I lean in to look inside. I see bits and pieces, nothing of value. The kind of treasure that children deem worthy but adult eyes would consider trash.

Jesus smiles at my thoughts.

Then He speaks: *"Child, this box hasn't been opened in a long time. You are carrying a lot of fear, pain, intimidation and hurt. But you don't need it anymore."*

As He says this, He begins to pull out each and every item. I can see the scars of the cross on His skin as He begins to clean out this ancient treasure chest that has been hiding within me.

In a moment, and without hesitation, He flings it all in the air. As He does, it disappears. It is gone forever.

He smiles at me.

Then, He reaches into His chest and pulls out His heart. I can see it - red, bulging, beating in His scarred hands. I can hear its pulse in my ears.

Then He comes towards me again. Leaning in, He puts His heart in my little Tin box and closes it. Then, He thrusts the box back into my chest.

All of a sudden, I feel overwhelming love.
Love for those I find hard to love.
Love for those I had not forgiven.
Love for myself.
I felt love the way Jesus loves.

Then a vision flashes before my eyes.

I see people I have found hard to love. When I looked at them, they were like children. And I felt His love for them and the ache in His heart for them.

Then, as suddenly as I was in this place and experiencing a new heart of love, I am transported to the top of a mountain. The Lord is beside me.

He unveils the nations of the earth before my eyes, and I feel His heart for the nations. *This love is overwhelming.*

I could hear His heart beating in my ears - it was in my chest beating to a rhythm at the same time as Jesus' heart in His chest. We were in time, in the same rhythm, our hearts waltzing together to the sound.

And I know I can never see, feel, or be the same ever again – now that my treasure chest carries the jewel of His heart.

13

The Ancient Future Place

He has called me up to this mountain many times before. I walked quickly, feeling the brisk air whipping against my cheekbones.

Although it was cold, it awakened my body and spirit with refreshing and expectation.

I was being summoned by the King.

These moors were hard to find. I would never be able to find it on my own. Yet I can come here when He calls me.

As I walked, I had confidence in each step, for it seemed an inner compass was directing me to these ancient ruins of redeeming grace. The place where Jesus was waiting for me. It was a magnetic pull: when the call came, I just knew where to go.

Instead of growing tired from the long walk, I was invigorated with every step as the life energy of Heaven drew me to the place where I would commune with my master.

The sky is overcast. The only sound I can hear is the wind and the rustling of my clothes against my hurried body. All I can see is green grass and more mountains. The expanse of land is enormous and spacious.

Eventually, as I look ahead, I can see the castle of the secret place. It looks abandoned, but it is not. Even though it is isolated, it is mine and my Beloved's castle, hidden only for us. It is the secret place.

As I get closer, I see the ancient brickwork on the walls and the flooring. Red-coloured bricks lovingly placed by hand by otherworldly beings in another lifetime. Built as He knew me, yet before I was born.

I walk through the archway into a courtyard. Here is a circular opening with green vines growing over the walls. Speckled with brilliant small white flowers with the sweetest perfume, they are drawn towards the gentle trickle of the waterfall in the courtyard's centre. It is a small circular well that springs forth the purest water. I drink from this well and look over the wall. I can see the wideness and spaciousness of the land below me. I am high above a planet, looking down. And I wait.

But I do not have to wait long.

Out of the wooden doorway that leads into the castle, Jesus walks towards me. He is robed in the most brilliant white robes. As He comes forth, glistening amongst the grey skies, the flowers begin to pulse with light.

All of nature sings when Jesus enters. Even the rocks cannot stay silent. There is rhythm and melody as the castle comes to life with His presence.

He walks towards me and opens his arms. At that moment, He embraces me. His robe envelopes my whole body. It heals me and breaks me at the same time. Tearing down walls I have built with the mortar of my pain and the bricks of my failures. He pulls back; I am also now covered in white robes. My travelling clothes are gone.

He puts his arm around me and looks over the land. He begins to talk to me about my life. I need not say a thing, as he knows my every thought. He speaks to the core of my troubles. He sings to the hidden desires of my heart. He tells me things about my future. He instructs me and gives me strategies. Answering every question and concern, I feel my body begin to relax. Words of life because He knows my past, and my present, yet He also knows my future.

The sky is beginning to set into dusk. The sun has peeked through the overcast clouds and birthed a pink hue that pierces through them. He points to the sky. As He does, a strange thing happens.

A clear computer screen covers the face of the sky, and Jesus begins to show me the course of action that will take place. Like a scene from mission impossible, he shows me statistics, references, names, people, and places.

He shows me songs, scriptures, and art. He swirls his hands over this screen like a great artisan, calling up ideas and dreams. It is frantic and creative, much like a painter who sees something in his mind and cannot paint it fast enough. He is calling dreams into reality.

That which seemed impossible is now becoming *mission possible.*

When He is finished, He embraces me again. I am full of Him and equipped by His love. I can now go, knowing I can visit again when I need or want to. I am always welcome here.

As I begin my walk home, I think of the many other times I have been saved by this secret place. It always starts the same way. I walk through the moors under a grey sky until I reach the courtyard.

At times He has sat me at a long wooden table with 12 chairs. Sometimes we eat and talk. He has given me a crystal glass goblet of which I drink the sweetest red liquid. It refreshes my palette and all my senses. At other times I have come as He held my unborn and uncreated longed for baby in His arms.

He hands him to me to cradle and tells me he will be here very soon. I get to see his face and feel his warmth. I am a new mother in this world and know that I will receive it when the time is right because of His promise.

Coronation Day

*A*re you ready for today?" My Lord speaks.

As Jesus anticipated my answer, I had not thought of why I was on this ship that soared the skies.

Floating effortlessly without the whirring of machinery past streams of clouds.

Defying human invention...
Created by supernatural blueprints...
Made from the master's hands.

I turned to face Him, "What is happening today?" I ask.

His laugh rang through the music of the wind.
"Your coronation day, of course!".

I didn't really know what that meant, but I was happy to trust He was leading me. It was so peaceful here, high up above the clouds. Nothing could touch me here.

I looked down at my clothes and realised I was not in everyday wear. Cloaked upon me was a white flowing dress. Made of what, I could not tell, but it was as smooth as the finest silk and possibly royal.

The air was of a summer morning, brushing on fabrics in the breeze, both my clothes and the rustic sails taking us further into the dawn sky.

As the boat rocked gently on the wind, a giant eagle soars alongside us. It came closer. Its wings spanning across the sunrise, also leaning on the breeze. His back held a harness and saddle. Yet he was not weary. This battle-worn beast wore silver scars like a king would wear jewellery - as part of his legacy and pride.

Up ahead, I saw a mountain. It was almost higher than the sky - surely no one could reach here unless the master allowed it. Carved into its peak was a rocky plain made flat - a pathway in the middle, trees on the side and beyond a forest of more mountains and foliage. Flowers spring from cracks and crevices- because all things can grow here.

Jesus looks at me and smiles. "Come on," He says as He adventurously jumps out of the boat and onto the feathered back of the eagle. He grabs the harness and waits for me to do the same.

I jump out of the boat to free-fall a short distance. As I land beside him, my bare feet, which have walked many distances, feel refreshed by the eagle's soft feathers. Underneath, I can feel the rhythm of its heartbeat, strong and brave.

Jesus leads us towards the mountain. As we get closer, I see people waiting. Standing in a two-line formation, they greet us as we softly land. Cheering us on as we leap off the saddle and onto the mossy ground.

I think I do not know who they are..... until I am closer.

Here are generations gone before me - passed from this life and onto the next - some five years, ten years, some one hundred years before.

Here, they are waiting for me? What is this? I think to myself. *Why am I here, and why are they so happy?*

I see my grandfather, with his piano accordion in his hands, singing to the folk sounds that emanate from its body. His dark, leathered face is shining.

My grandmother is beside him. She is younger, as is he; they are healthy and robust. She is clapping her hands to the rhythm, and her face is beaming.

I see my other nonna, laughing and clutching her hands - "*She's here!*" She says, "*She's finally here!*" She exclaims.

Jesus looks at me and smiles. He takes my hand and walks me down the aisle made between my ancestors.

As we reach the end of the plain, Jesus turns to me, and the crowd quietens. Jesus turns to face me.

"It is time, my daughter. It is time."

Around my waist is my battle sword. It has been with me in many trials. Held in its leather sheath, it has become part of me after all these years of war.

Jesus gently unbuckles it and takes it from me. *"You won't be needing this one anymore."*

Out of his robe, He pulls out a small silver dagger. Stunning and priceless. It is made of the most refined metal and marked by brilliant ancient carvings on its handle. Jewels embedded in sapphire blue and ruby red. Drawn from earth or Heaven's soil, I cannot tell.

"No longer do you fight an enemy you know from afar off," He says. *"This fight is up close and personal. It is reserved for the finest warriors. Those who are not afraid to walk into the enemy camp and into his personal chambers. You are ready for this fight."*

He places this new weapon around my waist.

Next, He holds in His hand a head wreath. Made of pure gold, it is adorned with flowers that glisten even in the faintest of light. He places it gently on my head.

How did I deserve this honour from the finest and noblest of kings? I do not know but humbly accept.

As the wreath gently rests on my head, it begins to mesh into my skin until it becomes a part of me.

"You are a royal daughter of the court. You have been adorned with a crown that only spiritual eyes can see. In your darkest trials, remember to open your eyes and remind yourself of who you really are and who you belong to. This crown makes you recognisable to kings and priests, but also to the spiritual savages. They lie in wait to destroy you. But they will always fail. They live in fear of your royal heritage. Do not forget who you are, for that is the key to winning every battle."

I bow my head to receive these words.

"Now, my child", He continues, *"I knight you as a warrior of my court."*

He picks up a large sword, centuries old. Reminding me of stories of King Arthur and knights of the round table, I bow in its shadow.

He places the sword on one shoulder and then the next, then kneels in front of me.

"My child, I place my authority in you. I place my identity in you. I give you my peace. Not as the world gives, but as I give. Do not fear what is ahead. These will be the greatest of days!"

He grabs my hands and lifts me to my feet. As He does, the great cloud of witnesses breaks into applause.

They begin to dance and sing.

They grab my hands and invite me to join the dance.

The great waltz in the clouds, alongside the eagle, the generations, the crown and the sword.

The dance of my coronation day.

Winter Hiding

Winter hides things.
But not to be deceitful.
Crisp air becomes the sheets that cover.

Snow, the blanket that conceals the rocks and the cracks.
Rain, the oxygen of regeneration.
The atmosphere becomes the bedding of a sleep chamber,
The place we go to close our eyes and rejuvenate.

It is dark. There is no motion.
Only rhythms of breathing as organs rest.
No consuming, no producing
Only dreaming.

And as morning light gently awakens the wombs of the dawn,
Eyes become wide open,
And imaginations of the night leak out from them.
Glistening pupils of majestic contemplations collide into reality.

We pull back the barren blankets to unveil a glorious sight...
In our slumber, things did not die.
The hiding grows the revealing.
And it is only then we realise,
Without the winter, there is no birth of spring.

"Next it dawned on him that the former ideas were of the world, the latter God-sent; finally, worldly thoughts began to lose their hold, while heavenly ones grew clearer and dearer."

— Ignatius of Loyola, The Spiritual Exercises of St. Ignatius of Loyola

Colossians 3:2 (MSG)

Don't shuffle along, eyes to the ground, absorbed with the things right in front of you. Look up, and be alert to what is going on around Christ—that's where the action is. See things from his perspective.

Ephesians 1:17-18 (ESV)

"...that the God of our Lord Jesus Christ, the Father of glory, may give you the Spirit of wisdom and of revelation in the knowledge of him, 18 having the eyes of your hearts enlightened, that you may know what is the hope to which he has called you..."

Roma Waterman is an award winning songwriter and author from Melbourne, Australia. With a heart to serve the body of Christ and a passion for prophetic and worship, Roma has been transforming lives around the world since her teens.

Her teachings on prophetic living, Christian spirituality, along with music, voice, and worship, have led her to reach people from all walks of life as they seek a closer relationship with Jesus. Her online school HeartSong Prophetic Alliance trains thousands around the world. Now, she's continuing her mission by sharing her story with more people who need to hear the life-changing message of the power of the Holy Spirit to radically transform hearts and lives. Roma is currently studying a Masters of Spirituality and resides in Melbourne, Australia, with her husband and two children. To find out more about Roma, please visit www.romawaterman.com

www.ingramcontent.com/pod-product-compliance
Lightning Source LLC
Chambersburg PA
CBHW020322010526
44107CB00054B/1944